Photography by:
Arthus Bertrand, Hugo van Lawick, Caroline Weaver,
Hans Reinhard, M.D. England, Adrian Warren,
Mitch Reardon, Leslie Groff, Alan Wearing,
P. Morries, ARDEA.

WILDEBEEST FAMILY

Jane Goodall

A MADISON MINI BOOK

Published by Madison Marketing Limited.
Madison Marketing Limited holds the exclusive
license to this edition.

ISBN 1-55066-020-9

Printed in Canada

Printed on recycled paper

WILDEBEEST FAMILY

Jane Goodall
ANIMAL SERIES

Photographs selected by
Michael Neugebauer

Madison Marketing Limited

Jacko, a wildebeest calf, has just been born. Within a few moments he is trying to stand. He tries again and again, but every time he's almost up, his long legs splay out in all directions and over he goes.

His mother keeps nudging him gently and often this makes him tumble down again. But the mother keeps on trying and the calf keeps on trying. And at last, just 10 minutes after being born, Jacko is on his feet. He takes a couple of steps and tries to suckle.
His mother jumps away and he falls. He gets up, more quickly this time, and once more tries to suckle. Again, his mother won't let him.

Another wildebeest comes to look at Jacko – very soon now she will have her baby. At last, when Jacko has walked many steps his mother stops so that he can suckle.

All over the great plains there are little calves like Jacko. There are also zebras and antelopes and ostriches. But mostly, there are wildebeests. The air is filled with the sound of their lowing, and their cow-like smell. The morning sun gleams on their white beards and on the fringe that hangs down from their necks.

In the distance a pack of wild dogs are chasing some wildebeests. Almost certainly they will catch a young one. Those who quickly learn to run are the most likely to survive.

Two young wildebeest bulls start to play. They leap into the air, then spin round and round.
They seem to be full of energy. It helps to keep them fit and strong. And the fittest and strongest will be the most successful fathers.

These two race off, then stop and pretend to fight, dropping onto thin knees with their horns clashing. Sometimes males fight quite fiercely – usually when they both want the same female.

While his mother grazes, Jacko stretches out on the ground and rests. But when she runs off, startled by a tourist car driving too fast, he is up in a flash and running after her. He is a strong fellow, this one. Soon all the wildebeests start moving eastward across the plain.

The wildebeests have to cross a small lake. They plunge in and start to swim. Even the calves can swim well. But there are so many animals milling about in the water that some of the youngsters get separated from their mothers. When they all reach the other side I hear many calves bleating sadly. Soon the right mothers and calves meet up. Sometimes, though, calves get quite lost and may die.

By evening Jacko is quite strong on his legs. He sucks lustily, butting his mother's flank.
Suddenly a young cheetah appears. She charges towards Jacko but his mother quickly chases her off. Jacko is lucky – if the cheetah had been fully grown he would probably have been killed.

It's the rainy season and the grass is green. Every time it rains, water collects in the hollows in the ground. And thousands of animals have come here. They stretch away as far as I can see.

For now Jacko is safe. But there are enemies everywhere and I know that some of the newborn wildebeests will be gone by morning. Still, there are so many calves that not all of them can be killed. Let's hope that little Jacko will be one of the survivors.

JANE GOODALL has shared her important discoveries and her love of animals with millions of people around the world through books, films and lectures. She has founded ongoing research and educational institutes on two continents, and is one of the world's most acclaimed naturalists.

The Jane Goodall Institute for Wildlife
Research, Education and Conservation
P.O. Box 41720, Tucson, AZ 85717 U.S.A.

The Jane Goodall Institute — Canada
P.O. Box 3125, Station "C"
Ottawa, Ontario K1Y 4J4 Canada

The Jane Goodall Institute — U.K.
15 Clarendon Park
Lymington, Hants S041 8AX United Kingdom